## PREFACE

There is a moment in time that has buried itself in my soul…nothing earthshattering, nothing very dramatic, but for whatever reason, it continues to be very clear in my memory. Every once in a while, this little moment surfaces and the whole scene, like a short video clip, plays out again in my mind.

I was in the $9^{th}$ grade in a small Catholic high school in the historic town of New Castle, Delaware. I was 14 years old and this event occurred when our pastor, Father Andrew White, came for his visit to the classroom to teach religion to the upper grades.

Allow me to digress first for a moment to give you more background. My parents were staunch Catholics. We attended Mass as a family every Sunday and recited the rosary every evening together. Crucifixes, statues, and holy cards were household items in the Schauber home.

We were somewhat poor but very content perhaps because there were sixteen children in the family and, trust me, there was never a dull moment.

The only two occasions in which we could hope to set foot in an actual restaurant would be to celebrate our First Communion or our Confirmation. My parents would take us out on those special days to the then Howard Johnson Restaurant with its iconic orange roof. It was a deeply treasured experience that provided the final touches to those two special Sacraments.

I was captivated by my father's evident holiness. As I caught glimpses of him kneeling at his bedside, deeply lost in his night prayer, I was so happy to have him as my father. When we were little, he would gather us around him in the evening to listen to the reading of a bible story and then he would question us on what we had heard. I loved those little gatherings.

With one of my older sisters, Henrietta, I had started going with Dad to the 6:30 Mass in the parish each morning. It was a precious time for me. When Henrietta, who was four years older than I, left to join the Marines, it was just Dad and I and I loved it. To be honest, I think I treasured those private moments with Dad as we drove into town more than anything else and I am ashamed to admit that I think the Mass was probably secondary in my teenage perspective. I was going to daily Mass more to have time with my father than to have quality time with Jesus. I think our heavenly Father must smile sometimes when He sees our foolishness and he loves us anyway.

Back to the video clip:

Father entered the classroom to begin his religion lesson. Those were the days when children stood anytime an adult entered the room and sat down only when we were told to do so. Father motioned us to be seated; he paused for what seemed several minutes. He certainly had our full attention as we waited for him to speak. When he did speak, he said something that touched me profoundly.

Without remembering his exact introduction, word for word, I can share with you what I do remember. Father said to us, slowly and with emphasis, "If any of you here in this classroom desires to become a saint, today I can give you the key to holiness."

All eyes were on him (those were indeed innocent times) but I held my breath wondering what this key to holiness could possibly be. He continued to look slowly around the room and seemed to be looking directly into the eyes of each student, one by one. At last he spoke again, "Today, we will learn about the Beatitudes, the key to holiness."

The Beatitudes…what a neat sounding word, I thought and, even more importantly, these Beatitudes held the key to holiness! I was impatient for Father to tell us more and he did. He began to recite each of the Beatitudes slowly, one by one.

"Blessed are the poor in spirit, for theirs is the kingdom of heaven; blessed are the merciful for they will obtain mercy, etc."

I didn't completely understand what each Beatitude meant at that moment, but it didn't matter to me. I was mesmerized by the fact that these eight Beatitudes were the key to holiness. I wanted very much to be holy because I could then be more like my father. I figured out that I would need to listen carefully during the next few classes as Father would explain and clarify the Beatitudes for us. I was genuinely captivated by the idea of a "key to holiness," at least for the moment.

Unfortunately, my little story is cut short here. I only remember up until the point where we had taken copious notes on these now famous Beatitudes and we were ready to move on in our religion curriculum.

In other words, I didn't follow through. I dropped the ball, the Beatitude-ball; that would pretty much sum it up. I think I must have lost interest because I don't remember much about Father's explanation of the eight Beatitudes. By the way, the word, *Beatitude*, translates into *blessing*, so they are sometimes referred to as the *blessings*.

Looking back, I think I just got busy with other things and the blessings went to the back of my mind and my heart. My dream to hold the key to holiness died and I continued along my life's journey busy with the many things that all teenagers become involved in; alas, the little flickering flame of joyous excitement got snuffed out and I can tell you with complete and absolute certainty and brutal honesty, I did not become holy, even with the promised aid of a "key to holiness."

Fast forward to now which is some fifty plus years later; I had been discerning God's will concerning the writing of this second book, a book on the Beatitudes, as understood and explained by St. Francis de Sales. It is as if now everything has finally and truly come full circle. I believe in my heart that God has been waiting patiently over these many, many years for the exact moment when he would re-awaken the mind and heart of that once overly excited teenager who is now a gently aging Oblate Sister of St. Francis de Sales, so grateful and happy to have this second chance.

I do indeed sense a feeling of holy excitement as I picture myself and the readers of this book exploring the Beatitudes under the tutelage of St. Francis de Sales and exploring this key to holiness to become the saints we are called to be. This time, I promise, I will not allow myself to become busy or to forget. With the printing of this book, I have committed myself completely to this task of walking through the Beatitudes with each of you. May the "blessings" captivate your heart and your soul and may each of us seek for authentic holiness. Jesus himself has told us that we must strive to *"be perfect, just as your heavenly Father is perfect"* (Matthew 5:48) and He has provided us the "key to holiness."

Jesus teaches the Beatitudes

# Foreword

Alexander T. Pocetto, OSFS
*De Sales University*

One day while driving, I heard a D.J. on the car radio say: "Happiness is not getting want you want, but wanting what you get." This bit of wisdom goes to the very heart of the Beatitudes. It runs contrary to what our consumerist society and culture constantly drum into our ears, viz., happiness consists in getting all we want and when we want it. When we get what we want, we are frequently disillusioned and unsatisfied. This dissatisfaction simply creates disordered desires and lives that leave many hungering and thirsting for something or someone beyond self-centeredness and self satisfaction.

Through bitter experience, we come to learn that true happiness or blessedness does not consist in getting what we want but what God wants. And what God wants is most clearly and concisely spelled out in the Beatitudes. St. Francis de Sales believed that we will never be holy according to our will but according to God's will. His will as enshrined in the beatitudes is certainly challenging and countercultural.

The Beatitudes as the saint taught and lived them help us to want what we get. They make us understand that there are many conditions, situations and events in our daily lives over which we have little or no control. When we face and accept what we get as coming from the loving hands of God, we trust and rely on his love and guidance. In this way we learn to joyfully live the way that Jesus lived. He lovingly accepted the hand that was dealt out to him by embracing unconditionally our human condition to please his beloved father. In all circumstances and situations, Jesus wanted what He got.

The great success of Sr. John Marie's previous book, *Salesian Pearls of Wisdom*, gives convincing evidence that there is a great hunger among the faithful to learn more about the spirituality of St. Francis de Sales and the many tried and true ways he points out to us for achieving holiness or blessedness. This present work, when carefully reflected on and lived, responds very effectively to this desire and will help us understand that "happiness is not getting what [we] want but wanting what [we] get."

## Introduction

If you happen to have read my first book, *Salesian Pearls of Wisdom*, you will be familiar with my style of writing. The style I am most comfortable with is that of two good friends chatting together, sharing insights and supporting each other in friendship and prayer.

We will therefore read small passages from the thoughts of St. Francis on a particular Beatitude and then I will pose questions, challenges, and insights that will help us to apply them to our state in life and the times in which we are living and, most importantly, to try to connect the Beatitude to your personal faith journey and where you are in your quest for holiness.

My sincere hope is that you will take our spiritual friendship seriously. Each day, I send a prayer and a blessing to heaven for anyone who might be reading either of my books on that day. I would deeply appreciate your prayers for me, as well. My dear friend, let us begin!

Keep this little book on your nightstand or on a shelf where you will always know where to find it. This book was never written to be read once and then packed away. Like my first book, it is meant to be a guide book, a book to turn to when you need some help. I hope you will come back to it often. God is truly asking you to go through the *narrow gate* that leads into the kingdom.

## Some Background on St. Francis

In his *Introduction to the Devout Life,* St. Francis addresses many of the Beatitudes. We will be drawing heavily from this book to walk with Francis through his teachings on each Beatitude. The *Introduction to the Devout Life* is mostly a compilation of letters that Francis wrote to Madame Louise de Charmoisy whose husband was the Duke of Savoy. She wanted Francis to assist her in her quest for holiness in the midst of the worldly life at the king's court. Since she lived at a distance, he gave her spiritual direction through letters that he sent to her, in response to questions she posed to him. She shared his letters with a Jesuit friend, Father Jean Fourier, who realized the wonderful benefit these could be for others and he persuaded Francis to allow them to be printed in book form. We owe a deep debt of gratitude to Madame de Charmoisy and to her Jesuit friend for bringing such a project to fruition, producing the classic book that has enthralled and continues to enthrall countless persons who are in search of holiness; since you are holding this book in your hands, my friend, I assume you are among them.

## Table of Contents

1st Beatitude – Blessed are the poor in spirit.
Page 17

2nd Beatitude – Blessed are those who mourn.
Page 24

3rd Beatitude – Blessed are the meek.
Page 31

4$^{th}$ Beatitude – Blessed are those who hunger and thirst for righteousness.
Page 37

5$^{th}$ Beatitude – Blessed are the merciful.
Page 47

6$^{th}$ Beatitude-Blessed are the pure of heart.
Page 53

7$^{th}$ Beatitude – Blessed are the peacemakers.
Page 60

8$^{th}$ Beatitude – Blessed are those who are persecuted for the sake of righteousness.
Page 69

## First Blessing

## *Blessed are the poor in spirit, for theirs is the kingdom of God.*

This first Beatitude has to do with wealth and poverty, sharing and not sharing, being rich in worldly goods but open to the needs of others. It has to do with being rich, but not being attached to riches. Have you known persons like that…persons who were wealthy but were also very generous in assisting those less fortunate? They are a true inspiration to those they help and they help without any fanfare. Theirs will surely be the Kingdom of Heaven because what they do to the least of their brothers, they do to Jesus. Francis shares his perspective on this first Beatitude:

*He is poor in spirit whose heart is not filled with the love of riches, whose mind is not set upon them. There is a wide difference between having poison and being poisoned. All apothecaries have poisons ready for special uses, but they are not consequently poisoned, because the poison is only in their shop, not in themselves; and so you may possess riches without being poisoned by them, so long as they are in your house or purse only, and not in your heart. It is the Christian's privilege to be rich in material things, and poor in attachment to them, thereby having the use of riches in this world and the merit of poverty in the next.*

*If you cleave closely to your possessions, and are encumbered with them, setting your heart and thoughts upon them, and restlessly anxious lest you should suffer loss, then, believe me, you are somewhat feverish; for fever patients drink the water we give them with an eagerness and satisfaction not common to those who are well.*

*Therefore, do not fix your longings on anything which you do not possess; do not let your heart rest in that which you have; do not grieve overmuch at the losses which may happen to you; then you may reasonably believe that although rich in fact, you are not so in affection, but that you are poor in spirit, and therefore blessed, for the Kingdom of Heaven is yours.* (*Introduction to the Devout Life,* excerpts from Part 3, Chapter 14, pp. 120-122)

We have much food for thought, my friend. I would like to break it down to four concepts that Francis speaks about in this first blessing:

1. He is poor in spirit whose heart is not filled with the love of riches, whose mind is not set upon them. It is neither good nor bad to be rich as long as our hearts are not set upon riches.
2. Do not let your heart rest in that which you have. Like poison, our riches must be in our house (or bank), or purse, but not trapped in our hearts.
3. We are privileged as Christians to be called to being poor in spirit...as was our Divine Master who modeled a simple and poor life style.
4. Do not grieve overmuch at the losses that may happen to you.

Let us pause for a moment and reflect on these quotes from Francis:

First, how well are we doing in not yearning for things we do not possess? Do we have a desire for the very latest gadget and gizmo that comes across our television screen or flat screen? Do we struggle with purchasing things we don't need but we certainly want? If we were to do an apparel inventory of all of our clothing...what would we find? I believe Francis is telling us to take a close look at these issues and go deeply into our hearts to make sure they are not weighed down by a love for possessions.

Second, is it possible that we have allowed Francis' metaphorical poison to enter into our heart? I think it can happen subtly over time, almost without our knowing it. We will know the answer if we ponder within ourselves these questions: Do I freely give when an occasion arises, such as a collection for the homeless? Do I give generously, according to my means, in the Mass collection in my church? Have I made an effort to support two or three special causes that touch my heart? I cannot give to every request that arrives in the mail, but I can gently commit myself to the ones I will generously embrace and support.

Third, we have Christ as our model of living simply, totally unencumbered by concerns for amassing money. He even had to borrow a coin from someone else to make his point to the Pharisees about paying the tax to Caesar. It might be good to sit quietly in his presence now and ask His opinion on our lifestyle and our willingness to reach out to others in acts of kindness and support. If we meditate on the life of Jesus as portrayed by the scriptures, we learn that money is not the only gift we should share. We also need to be joyfully available, for example, for volunteering for tutoring, serving in soup kitchens, or working in social outreach programs. What we do to the least of our brethren, we do to our beloved Jesus.

Last, if we find ourselves overly grieving for a monetary loss or a loss of some material thing, we may need to spend time with the Lord about this. It could be a sign that we are too attached to those things.

My dear friend, I hope I did not appear to be too harsh or judgmental in the thoughts I posed for your consideration. I deeply desire that this book might be an authentic path to holiness for you, and holiness can only come about if we go deep within ourselves and cleanse our hearts of all that is an obstacle to true holiness.

There are some serious questions we must ask ourselves and we could become discouraged with this project of seeking to be holy. Please don't give up; sit quietly and gently in the presence of Jesus and let him help you and encourage you and guide you…he seeks holiness for you far more than you seek it. He knows the rewards in the Kingdom for those who are *poor in spirit*. He is holding you in his loving embrace and I am holding you in prayer. You are carried in my heart and in my prayers as we move, when you are ready, to the next blessing.

## Second Blessing

## *Blessed are those who mourn, for they will be comforted.*

It is to Benedict XVI that we turn to get an introduction to this second blessing. He will shed some consoling light as we are introduced to the second Beatitude. In a talk given in 2007, he addressed the meaning of *mourning*. Read his commentary carefully; his message is profound:

*Let us go back to the second beatitude: Blessed are those who mourn, for they shall be comforted. Is it good to mourn and to declare mourning blessed? There are two kinds of mourning. The first is the kind that has lost hope, that has become mistrustful of love and of truth and that therefore eats away and destroys man from within. But there is also the mourning occasioned by the shattering encounter with truth which leads man to undergo conversion and to resist evil. This mourning heals, because it teaches man to hope and to love again.*

*Judas is an example of the first kind of mourning: struck with terror at his own fall, he no longer dares to hope and hangs himself in despair. Peter is an example of the second kind: struck by the Lord's gaze, he bursts into healing tears that plow up the soil of his soul. He begins anew and is himself renewed. (Jesus of Nazareth,* p. 86*)*

Now we move back to St. Francis de Sales and his teachings on the Second Beatitude: *blessed are those who mourn.* I was unable to find any actual quotes from him on this Beatitude, but Francis has some beautiful teachings on sadness and suffering. Sadness and suffering do, indeed, send us into an interior mourning; so we will draw from his thoughts on sadness and suffering to get a fuller understanding of this Beatitude. In his *Introduction to the Devout Life*, he has the following to say about sorrow.

*"Godly sorrow produces a salutary repentance without regret,"* says St. Paul, *"but worldly sorrow produces death"* (2 Corinthians 7:10).

*Sorrow may be good or bad according to the several results it produces in us. The Enemy makes use of sadness to try good men with his temptations – just as he tries to make bad men merry in their sin, so he seeks to make the good sorrowful amid their works of piety.*

*If ever such sadness comes upon you, make use of the following remedy: "Is anyone among you suffering? He should pray," says St. James* (James 5:13).

*The worldly sorrow disturbs the heart, plunges it into anxiety, stirs up unreasonable fears, disgusts it with prayer, overwhelms and stupefies the brain, deprives the soul of wisdom, judgment, resolution and courage, weakening all its powers; in a word, it is like a hard winter, blasting all the earth's beauty, and numbing all animal life for it deprives the soul of sweetness and power in every faculty.*

*Should you, my child, ever be attacked by this evil spirit of sadness, make use of the following remedies: Prayer is a sovereign remedy, it lifts the mind to God who is our only Joy and Consolation. But when you pray let your words and affections, whether interior or exterior, all tend to love and trust in God.*

*Vigorously resist all tendencies to melancholy, and although all you do may seem to be done coldly, wearily and indifferently, do not give in. Make use of hymns and spiritual songs; it is well also to occupy yourself in external works with as much variety as may lead us to divert the mind from the subject which oppresses it.*

*Lay bare all the feelings, thoughts and longings that are the result of your depression to your confessor or director, in all humility and faithfulness; seek the society of spiritually-minded people, and frequent such as far as possible while you are suffering.* (*Introduction to the Devout Life,* excerpts from Part 4, Chapter 12, pp. 204-206).

27

And so, my dear friend, Francis has taught us in all these strategies to learn to walk through our sorrow, our suffering, our sadness and mourning. It is only in walking through it while holding tightly to the hand of our heavenly Father that the Beatitude can bring its reward: *for they will be comforted.*

This was a very challenging Beatitude and we need to spend some time digesting the deep truths we encountered.

I will do as before and extract the main points of this Beatitude; that should help us in our understanding of how we, as followers of Jesus, must learn from His own deep sufferings and His total surrender to the Father's will.

Pope Benedict explains the concept of two kinds of mourning: one that heals us and another that destroys us. Spend some quiet time with both Judas and Peter…there is so much to learn from their actions.

St. Francis confirms Benedict's statement that there are two kinds of sorrow, depending on what each sorrow does to our soul. Giving in to the *evil spirit of sadness* can drain our courage and our trust. Francis has no qualms in talking about the role that Satan plays in our periods of sorrow and sadness. His graphic description of sorrow and sadness as the blast of a brutal and deadly winter is a powerful image. Sit quietly with Jesus as you ponder all these teachings of Francis. As you look back on times in your life when you were experiencing a deep sadness, was it a sadness that destroyed or a sadness that came to healing? As we each address challenges in the future, let us resolve to put ourselves immediately in a place of deep healing through prayer.

Francis does not leave his followers to fend for themselves. He gives plentiful suggestions and strategies to get us through the sorrow: *sing spiritual canticles, stay busy with work that is productive, pray earnestly, spend time with spiritually-minded people, confide in your confessor or spiritual director*. Spend time with each of these suggestions; do any resonate with your heart?

Last, turn to prayer as your best resource when the burden of sadness or sorrow invades your soul. Even if you have no feelings and your prayer seems dry and useless…do not quit. Prayer recited in dryness is far more valuable than prayer recited when your soul is in joy and consolation. And always keep in mind that the Beatitude does not end with mourning because Jesus has affirmed: Blessed are they who mourn, *for they will be comforted.* That comfort may not happen in this life; however, it is guaranteed for the next.

## Third Blessing

## *Blessed are the meek, for they will possess the earth.*

We live in a world that doesn't openly value meekness. In fact, meekness is often interpreted as being weak and lacking in the ability to take a stand. For that reason, we will use the word *gentle* to capture the fuller meaning of this beautiful Beatitude.

Wars are rampant around the globe; gangs and violence are out of control in our cities, and human trafficking looms as a dark shadow in our world, for just a few examples. In society today, we have even coined a new phrase that is familiar to all of us, but didn't even exist 20 years ago - "road rage." We are desperately in need of guidance to bring some gentleness to our world. In this Beatitude, Jesus doesn't just encourage us to strive for gentleness, but He actually asks that we look to Him; He wants to be our teacher: "Learn from me that I am meek and humble of heart" (Matthew 11:29). This Beatitude must be very special to Jesus for Him to offer Himself as the model. Francis also offers us many wonderful teachings to help us live out our lives in an authentic and steadfast spirit of gentleness and meekness.

Let us see what he has to say to us:

*The holy and illustrious Joseph while sending his brothers from Egypt back to his father's house gave them only this one advice: "Do not quarrel on the way"* (Genesis 45:24).

*I say the same to you: this miserable life is but the road to the blessed life to come. Therefore, let us not be angry at all with one another on the way. Let us walk in the company of our brothers and companions gently, peacefully and kindly. Further, I tell you plainly and without any exception: do not become angry at all if that is possible. Do not accept any pretext whatsoever to open the door of your heart. St. James says bluntly and without reservation that the anger of*

# Prayer Of St. Francis Of Assisi

Lord, make me an instrument of Thy peace; where there is hatred, let me sow love; where there is injury, pardon; where there is doubt, faith; where there is despair, hope; where there is darkness, light; and where there is sadness, joy.

O Divine Master, grant that I may not so much seek to be consoled as to console; to be understood as to understand; to be loved, as to love: for it is in giving that we receive, it is in pardoning that we are pardoned, and it is in dying that we are born to eternal life.

*man does not work the justice of God.* (James 1:20).

St. Francis quotes St. Augustine as having written to a friend: *"It is better to refuse entrance to even the least semblance of anger, however just, and that because once entered in, it is hard to be got rid of, and what was but a little mote soon waxes into a great beam* (*Introduction to the Devout Life,* excerpts from Part 3, Chapter 8, p. 110).

He advises us on how to attempt to control our anger when we find ourselves becoming agitated.

*When we feel stirred with anger, we ought to call upon God for help, like the Apostles when they were tossed about with wind and storm, and He is sure to say, "Peace, be still."* (Matthew: 8:24). *For he will command our passions to be still and there will be a great calm. But even here I would again warn you, that your very prayers against the angry feelings which urge you, should be gentle and calm and without vehemence.*

*Further, when you are conscious of an angry act, atone for the fault by some speedy act of gentleness toward the person who excited your anger. Moreover when there is nothing to stir your wrath, lay up a store of gentleness and kindness, speaking and acting in things great and small as gently as possible.* (*Introduction the Devout Life*, excerpts from Part 3, Chapter 8, pp.108-111).

We have certainly been given some powerful guidelines and strategies to use as we attempt to keep gentleness and meekness in our lives and the lives of our loved ones.

Some things to ponder:

Francis admits that it is better to live without anger than to try to control it after we have opened the door to anger. He reminds us through St. Augustine - once in, the small mote (a tiny splinter) grows into a great beam.

He encourages us to build up a provision of gentleness when we are at peace and without any anger.

He encourages us to turn to God as the Apostles did in the raging storm. He will calm the storm within.

Simply sit with all of this in the quiet of your heart and choose *gentleness* as your hallmark, your shield, and your mission. You will possess your own soul and you will possess the earth! It may not be the earth of this life, but the earth of the kingdom where there will be no anger, no hatred, no suffering or pain, only peace and harmony, bathed in love.

When I look back to the times when I have really shown an outburst of anger, I find myself regretting those moments. After we have spoken in anger, it is very difficult to take it back. Your opponents will remember your angry words; they will hardly have heard your apology or your attempt to rectify the situation; it is the angry words that will sear their hearts. Sit with this for a while…many sincere and good friendships have been shattered by angry words.

If you have young children, be especially careful in showing anger when you must correct them for something. A gentle rebuke will be much more effective than an abusive tirade.

Finally, recall how many times Jesus would have reason to be angry with us for some sin we have committed, some selfish deed we have done. Remember the prodigal son in the Gospel (Luke 15: 11-32): we need only return with a contrite and loving heart, and it is as if our heavenly Father has been watching and waiting and has already pardoned us even before we have started crawling back to ask his forgiveness. Be careful, though, there is a caveat: He will withhold this forgiveness from us if we are not willing to forgive those who have offended us. My dear, friend, let us strive to be gentle and meek. It is a beautiful way of life!

## Fourth Blessing

## *Blessed are those who hunger and thirst for righteousness, for they will be satisfied.*

At first glance, this Beatitude could cause a little confusion because of the word *righteousness*. It is not a word that is common in our everyday conversation. Therefore, what are we hungering and thirsting for in this Beatitude? We might have a vague sense of someone being righteous, but I think we would probably be more comfortable with descriptive words like: *just, holy, faithful*. In the beginning of this book, I introduced you to my father. I would never have thought to describe him as righteous; I most surely saw him as being holy.

The Jews, however, listening to Jesus on the mountainside that day, would have had a clear understanding of what Jesus was talking about. In the first book of the Bible, their forefather, Abraham, believed the words of God attesting to his future fatherhood over a great nation. Abraham had no offspring and, at the time of God's promise, was in his 90s. Abraham still believed that nothing was impossible with God, and this faith in God was credited to him by God as righteousness or as we would say holiness; holiness boils down to doing the will of God. The word *righteousness* shows up 238 times in the scriptures and every pious Jew, in Jesus' day wanted to be righteous, that is, faithful, obedient to the will of God, and prayerful, as Abraham was in his walk with God. In fact, the Greek word that Matthew used for righteousness, *Dikaiosune*, translates into *living in accordance with God's will*.

Jesus is calling us to hunger and thirst after holiness, and holiness in the teachings of St. Francis de Sales equates to doing always the will of God. In his Golden Counsels, we read:

*Here is the most important point: find out what God wants and, when you know, try to carry it out cheerfully or at least courageously; not only that, but you must love this will of God and the obligations it entails, even if it means performing the most menial tasks in the world the rest of your life, because whatever "sauce" God chooses for us, it should be all the same to us. In this practice lies the very bull's-eye of perfection at which we must all aim, and whoever comes the nearest to it wins the prize. Be of good will, I beg you; little by little train your will to follow God's will, wherever it may lead you; see that your will is strongly roused when your conscience says: God wants this.* (Golden Counsels, p.12)

Now that we are all on the same page with the vocabulary of the Beatitude, let us turn to St. Francis de Sales and hear his words on seeking holiness. Actually, first, I need to clear up one more word. Francis often equates holiness with the word *devout* (adjective) or *devotion* (noun). He even titled his book, *The Introduction to the Devout Life.* So, keep in mind as we explore this Fourth Beatitude that we are really talking about and referring to holiness.

I am going to handle this Beatitude a little differently. Francis was well versed in his understanding of what authentic holiness is. He was also one of the first to point out that holiness is for everyone, without exception. In his time, most people felt that holiness was for priests and religious only. Ordinary lay people, they believed, couldn't possibly find the time and help they needed if they were to embrace holiness. They also imagined that holiness meant harsh penances and fasting and long hours of prayer. St. Francis, in his book, tried to dispel all these false assumptions and introduced a holiness that was gentle and based on love of God and a spirit of compassionate kindness and service to each neighbor.

In his *Introduction to the Devout Life,* he points out to his readers what true holiness is and what false holiness is; he meticulously describes the steps to acquiring holiness. He points out the various roadblocks, the progression, and the encouragement needed for beginning the journey as well as the effort needed to continue the pursuit of holiness even in the midst of weakness and failures.

Keep in mind also that Jesus uses the words: "Blessed are those who hunger and thirst…" He places a certain urgency on the Beatitude. He doesn't want us to just think about holiness; He wants us to yearn for it with passion as we yearn for food when we feel desperately hungry and for drink when we desire deeply a cool drink of water. As I wrote earlier, He desires our holiness far more than we do, for he knows its reward both in this life and in the next.

We are going to have a quick lesson on holiness, by simply and quietly digesting St. Francis' exquisite thoughts and sayings on this topic. I encourage you to read the *Introduction to the Devout Life* if you feel so inclined or if you would like a more thorough understanding of this topic. For us now, I believe that a gentle walk through his words of wisdom will be the most fulfilling and the most beneficial to our souls. Quiet your mind and your body but keep your heart alert as you begin to savor these thoughts; somewhere in this litany of wisdom, there is one (or more) that is meant specifically for you. I found these quotes by typing into my Google browser: *quotes from St. Francis de Sales on the will of God* or *quotes from St. Francis de Sales on peace,* etc. I found a treasure trove of wonderful quotes that I hope will resonate with your heart. God is speaking through his beloved St. Francis de Sales.

1. *Abide steadfastly in your determination to cling simply to God, trusting in his eternal love for you.*

2. *Doing ordinary things in an extraordinary way is a great thing.*

3. *I have no doubt that God is holding you by the hand; if he allows you to stumble, it is only to let you know that if he were not holding your hand, you would fall. This is how he gets you to hold tighter to his hand.*

*4. Just as wherever birds fly, they always fly through the air; so also, wherever we go or wherever we are, we find God present.*

*5. Happy are they who walk in the way of God's love; their hearts are changed.*

*6. Belong totally to God. Think of Him and He will think of you. He has drawn you to Himself so that you may be His. He will take care of you.*

*7. First thing in the morning, prepare your heart to be at peace; then take great care throughout the day to call it back to that peace frequently, as it were, to again take your heart in your hand.*

*8. If the consideration of your weakness troubles you, cast yourself upon God and trust in him.*

*9. Let us walk with God, not considering where we are going, but with whom.*

*10. We can never love our neighbor too much. There is nothing small in the service of God.*

*11. Be patient with everyone, but above all with yourself.*

*12. A thousand times a day, cast your whole heart, your soul, your anxiety on God with great confidence, and say with the psalmist, I am yours, Lord. Save me.*

*13. Avoid anxieties and worries, for nothing else so impedes our progress toward perfection.*

*14. Most important, don't lose heart. Be patient, wait, do all you can to develop a spirit of compassion.*

*15. Let your heart be full of courage and your courage full of confidence in God.*

*16. Remember that the present day is given to you so that you may gain the future day of eternity. Make a firm purpose to use this day well.*

*17. Take care not to let yourself be moody or out of humor with those about you.*

*18. When the shore is gained, who will remember the toil and storm?*

I specifically chose the thoughts that seem to resonate with our quest for holiness. I suggest that you choose the one that touches your heart the most. Copy it on a little note card and carry it with you as your very special mantra on your path to holiness.

When you have made progress with that chosen quote, feel free to come back to the list and see if perhaps a different quote now touches your heart; choose it and carry it with you and recite it often to fill your heart with the wisdom St.

Francis has left for us, and to experience the joy that is found in living a devout and holy life.

## Fifth Blessing

## *Blessed are the merciful, for mercy will be shown them.*

As we move along on our Beatitude journey, I hope you are finding things that touch your heart deeply, and urge you on to really start living these blessings.

The next blessing concerns mercy. Let us start by thinking of what comes to our minds when we hear this Beatitude. I think we would probably be on the same page in our description of mercy. Mercy means, for example, forgiving someone. It often involves feeling pity and sympathy for someone and wanting to ease their pain or sorrow; it means pardoning someone and cancelling any punishment due to that person. I am sure we have all known a merciful person, perhaps a parent, a grandparent, a friend.

Jesus modeled mercy for us on many occasions: He pardoned sinners and freed them from their own sinfulness. Recall the woman taken in adultery. Jesus refused to condemn her; He pardoned her and encouraged her to sin no more (John 8:3-11). He felt sorry for the paralytic who was lowered through the roof; He first pardoned his sins, and only then performed the miracle on his body (Matthew 9:2-7). The most poignant incident of His bestowing mercy was during His passion when, under the most extreme suffering imaginable, He managed to cry out, "Father, forgive them; they know not what they do" (Luke 23:34).

St. Francis de Sales has a quote that has intrigued me for many years: he has said regarding mercy, "Our misery should be the throne of God's mercy" (*Golden Counsels*, p.11).

St. Francis tells us in essence that the measure of our misery is the measure of His mercy: the greater our misery, the greater is His mercy. The part that confuses me is the mention of *the throne of His mercy*. A throne is typically a very elegant, well-placed chair reserved only for the King. I am not quite sure what it means for our weakness to be his throne. If you have any insights, please send them to me. I would love to share in the wisdom you may have about this quote.

But as to God's infinite mercy, there is no confusion in my mind. I have experienced that mercy countless times in my life, especially after a reverent and faith-filled reception of the Sacrament of Reconciliation. I have experienced it in the gift of compassion and forgiveness others have shown toward me.

Perhaps the best way we can learn to live this beautiful Beatitude is to simply imbue our hearts with the gentle and inspiring words that St. Francis has given about forgiveness. As we did for the fourth Beatitude, let us read prayerfully, reverently, and with the desire to absorb and live out St. Francis de Sales' thoughts on mercy and forgiveness. Once more, be convinced that one of these thoughts is specifically for you. Treasure it and make it, or a part of it, your daily mantra. I would like to share with you the source of the quotes you are going to ponder. In my office at DeSales University, we have a networked printer. All staff members may use the printer and then go to the main office to pick up the printed document when it is convenient. I had just sent something to the printer one day and when I went to get my document, I found that someone had printed 50 copies of a sheet of thoughts from St. Francis de Sales. I wrote a little note asking if I could use those quotes for this Beatitude. I waited three or four days but no one responded to my request and the stack of 50 papers was right where I had found it. Finally, after waiting a little longer and still getting no response, I decided that St. Francis de Sales somehow arranged this specifically for my book; what I was freely given, I freely share with you.

*Keep yourself faithfully in the presence of God; avoid hurry and anxiety, for there are no greater obstacles to our progress in perfection. Have an unlimited confidence in His mercy and goodness.*

*Beware of yielding to any kind of distrust, for the heavenly goodness does not permit you to fall in order to abandon you, but to humble you and teach you to keep a firmer hold on to the hand of his mercy.*

*When we are in doubt of not having done our duty, or of having offended God, we must humble ourselves, beg God to forgive us, and start afresh. Pure love of God says to us: "Unfaithful one, humble thyself, rely upon the mercy of God, ask pardon, and after renewed promises of fidelity and love, continue on in the pursuit of perfection."*

*Let us keep firm hold of the merciful hand of our good God, for He wishes to draw us after him. Let us always keep on; however slow our progress, we are getting over a great deal of the road. God wishes that our misery should be the throne of His mercy.*

*Do like little children; while they feel their mother holding them by the sleeve, they go on boldly and run about everywhere, nothing daunted by the falls that are caused by the weakness of their legs. Thus, while God holds you by your good will to serve him, go on boldly, undaunted by your little stumblings.*

My dear friend, we have so many points to ponder here especially for those of us who may possibly find being merciful very challenging. Sometimes, the hurt done to us is so deep that forgiving might seem impossible. Please take your time and come back to this treasury of wisdom often to gain new courage and insights on the road to holiness.

We also need to recall that Jesus has made it very clear that if we are unwilling to show mercy to others, we cannot expect that He will show mercy to us. In the parable of the Unforgiving Servant, the king who had pardoned his servant's debt out of compassion, had no pity on him when he found out how harshly he treated a fellow servant who owed him a very small amount. The king handed him over to the torturers until he paid the whole debt. The last sentence from the parable is worth our reflection: "So will my heavenly Father do to you, unless each of you forgives his brother from his heart" (Matthew 18: 35.)

## Sixth Blessing

***Blessed are the pure of heart, for they shall see God.***

What does it mean to be pure of heart? Francis had a deep affection for purity of heart; he found it to be the virtue that makes us most like angels. In his mind, it had to do with being chaste, honest, transparent, and ultimately loving with a pure love.

I think it can also refer to persons who are childlike in their deep relationship with God; they are innocent and trusting and they see themselves as children of God. Their relationship with God is very much like a relationship between a loving Father and an obedient and trusting child.

St. Theresa of the Child Jesus had just such a relationship and was truly pure of heart. Mother Teresa of Calcutta is another beautiful example of this purity of heart.

The quotes that you will read in this Beatitude deal with the vocation to the single life, the married life, and the widowed life in the hope that his words will be of help to you in whatever vocation you are living out at this point in your life.

*Purity is the lily among virtues - by it men approach to the Angels. There is no beauty without purity, and human purity is chastity. We speak of the chaste as honest, and of the loss of purity as dishonor; purity is an intact thing, its converse is corruption. Its special glory is in the spotless whiteness of soul and body.*

*Close your heart to every questionable tenderness or delight, guard against all that is unprofitable though it may be lawful.*

*Everyone has great need of this virtue: those living in widowhood need a brave chastity not only to forego present and future delights, but also to resist the memories of the past. While fruits are whole, you may store them up securely, some in straw, some in sand or amid their own foliage, but once bruised there is no means of preserving them. Even so the purity which has never been tampered with may well be preserved to the end, but when once that has ceased to exist nothing can ensure its existence.*

*The unmarried need a very simple sensitivity to purity, which will drive away all over-curious thoughts. The young are apt to imagine that of which they are ignorant to be wondrous sweet, and as the foolish moth hovers around a light, and, persisting in coming too near, perishes in its inquisitive folly, so they perish through their unwise approach to forbidden pleasures.*

*And married people need a watchful purity whereby to keep God ever before them, and to seek all earthly happiness and delight through Him alone, ever remembering that He has sanctified the state of holy matrimony by making it the type of His own union with the Church.*

*The Apostle says, "Follow peace and holiness, without which no man shall see the Lord"*

(Hebrews 12:14*), by which holiness he means purity. Of a truth, my child, without purity no one can ever see God* (Matthew 5:8), *nor can any hope to dwell in His tabernacle except he lead an uncorrupt life* (Psalm 15:2); *and our Blessed Lord Himself has promised the special blessing of beholding Him, to those that are pure in heart.*

For our purposes, I prefer to think of *purity of heart* as an attitude, a way of life, no matter what state in life is ours at this time. It has to do with the description that I suggested earlier: utter transparency, honesty, and a childlike trust in our heavenly Father. Purity of heart is grounded in this deep relationship with God; God becomes the filter through which we love. We love our spouse, our children, our colleagues, our neighbor more deeply, because we love God deeply; and, for His sake, we try to keep our heart pure. We are careful of what we choose to read or to see on television, or at the movies.

## Preserving Purity

Francis not only shows us the beauty of purity of heart; he also teaches how to preserve this purity in our hearts. We need his wisdom more than ever because we live in a culture that uses sexual activity as entertainment in books, movies, television shows, and advertisements. Let us absorb the words of our gentle saint who was most assuredly pure of heart.

*Be exceedingly quick in turning aside from the slightest thing leading to impurity, for it is an evil that approaches stealthily, and in which the very smallest beginnings are apt to grow rapidly. It is always easier to fly from such evils than to cure them.*

*Human bodies are like glasses, which cannot come into collision without risk of breaking or like fruits, which, however fresh and ripe, are damaged by pressure. Never permit any one to take any manner of foolish liberty with you, since, although there may be no evil intention, the perfectness of purity is injured thereby.*

*St. Paul says without any hesitation that impurity and uncleanness, or foolish and unseemly talking, are not to be so much as named among Christians.* (Ephesians 5:3-4), *and all evil thoughts or foolish acts of levity or heedlessness are as steps towards the most direct breaches of the law of chastity.*

*Avoid the society of persons who are wanting in purity, especially if they are bold, as indeed impure people always are. On the other hand, seek out good and pure men, read and ponder holy things; for the Word of God is pure, and it will make those pure who study it: wherefore David likens it to gold and precious stones.* (Psalm 119:127).

*Always abide close to Jesus Christ Crucified, both spiritually in meditation and actually in Holy Communion; if you rest your heart upon Our Dear Lord, pure and immaculate, you will find that soon both heart and soul will be purified. (Introduction to the Devout Life*: excerpts from Part 3, Chapter 12 and 13).

Francis is firm and clear on his warnings and suggestions for being pure and maintaining a pure heart. The question we need to pose to ourselves is this: how important is this Beatitude to me? How much do I yearn to be *pure of heart*? If you truly desire purity of heart, then nurture this desire and surrender to it. I think Jesus delights in those who have chosen this blessing and are faithful to nurturing it in little ways each day. St. John, the beloved apostle, most assuredly was pure of heart. His love was so pure and so ardent for Jesus, that he could lay his head on the bosom of his beloved friend.

*There was reclining on Jesus' breast one of His disciples, whom Jesus loved* (John 13:23)

## Seventh Blessing

## *Blessed are the peacemakers for they will be called children of God.*

We come to our seventh Beatitude which offers the reward of being true children of our heavenly Father, children in whom he delights.

The guiding theme of this blessing will be based on this premise: we cannot be a peacemaker if peace is not first in our own heart. We cannot give what we do not have and we cannot be peacemakers without being at peace within ourselves.

First, we will explore an obstacle to peace. St. Francis de Sales would probably put this obstacle at the top of the list - anxiety. When we are anxious and worried and fearful, peace cannot be present within us. We need to rid ourselves of all anxiety and worry and fear and then peace can return.

Jesus gave a gentle rebuke to Martha, one of his closest friends, when he said to her, "Martha, Martha, you are anxious and worried about many things...only one thing is necessary. Mary has chosen the better part and it shall not be taken away from her" (Luke 10:41-42).

So, let us ponder the thoughts of St. Francis de Sales on this topic of anxiety. And let us allow St. Francis to lead us from the anxiety that saps our energy and destroys our peace to the blessing of learning to surrender gently and putting all our trust in God.

*This anxiety is the greatest evil that can happen to the soul, sin only excepted. Just as internal commotions and seditions ruin a commonwealth, and make it incapable of resisting its foreign enemies, so if our heart be disturbed and anxious, it loses power to retain such graces as it has, as well as strength to resist the temptations of the Evil One, who is all the more ready to fish (according to an old proverb) in troubled waters.*

*Anxiety arises from an unregulated desire to be delivered from any pressing evil, or to obtain some hoped-for good. Nevertheless nothing tends so greatly to enhance the one or retard the other as over-eagerness and anxiety. Birds that are captured in nets and snares become inextricably entangled therein, because they flutter and struggle so much. Therefore, whence you urgently desire to be delivered from any evil, or to attain some good thing, strive above all else to keep a calm, restful spirit - steady your judgment and will, and then go quietly and easily after your object. By easily I do not mean carelessly, but without eagerness, disquietude or anxiety; otherwise, so far from bringing about what you wish, you will hinder it, and add more and more to your perplexities.*

*Examine yourself often, at least night and morning, as to whether your soul is in your hand, or whether it has been wrested thence by any passionate or anxious emotion. See whether your soul is fully under control, or whether it has not in any way escaped from beneath your hand, to plunge into some unruly love, hate, envy, lust, fear, vexation or joy. And if it has so strayed, before all else seek it out, and quietly bring it back to the Presence of God, once more placing all your hopes and affections under the direction of His Holy Will. Just as one who fears to lose some precious possession holds it tight in his hand, so, like King David, we ought to be able to say, "My life is always in my hand, and yet do I not forget Thy Law"* (Ps. 119:109).

*Do not allow any wishes to disturb your mind under the pretext of their being trifling and unimportant, for if they gain the day, greater and weightier matters will find your heart more accessible to disturbance. When you are conscious that you are growing anxious, commend yourself to God, and resolve steadfastly not to take any steps whatever to obtain the result you desire, until your disturbed state of mind is altogether quieted*

*If you can lay your anxiety before your spiritual guide, or at least before some trusty and devout friend, you may be sure that you will find great solace. The heart finds relief in telling its troubles to another; it is the best of remedies, and it was what Saint Louis counseled his son, "If thou hast any uneasiness lying heavy on thy heart, tell it forthwith to thy confessor, or to some other pious person, and the comfort he will give will enable thee to bear it easily."* (*Introduction to the Devout Life*, excerpts from Part 4, Chapter 11).

## *Be at Peace!*

*Be at Peace*

*Do not look forward in fear to the changes of life;*

*Rather look to them with full hope that as they arise, God, whose very own you are, will lead you safely through all things.*

*And when you cannot stand, God will carry you in his arms.*

*Do not fear what may happen tomorrow.*

*The same everlasting Father who cares for you today will take care of you today and every day.*

*He will either shield you from suffering or will give you unfailing strength to bear it.*

*Be at peace and put aside all anxious thoughts and imaginations.*

Don't hesitate to return to this prayer every time you feel your trust weakening or your anxiety increasing. Let Francis lead you to a place of peace. Hold on tightly to our Father's hand at these moments. It is only when we possess true peace in our hearts that we can be peacemakers.

Nurture peace in your family, your home, your neighborhood, as well as in your workplace, your community, and even in your church.

Let us strive to be true peacemakers who, by gentle quiet deeds, generous acts of kindness, and great love for the person in front of us at any given moment, will plant seeds of peace and kindness and compassion wherever we are.

I am just going to share a few insights on this whole question of being at peace:

This peace cannot be based only on emotions. It must ultimately come from our will. We have to will to accept whatever suffering or difficulty the Father has planned for us in His infinite wisdom.

If we rely on our feelings and emotions, we are leaning on a very fragile support because emotions are unpredictable and changing. It is our will that must be in control. We need the same steadfastness that Jesus displayed in the Garden of Olives before His passion. His fear and dread were such that He even begged his Father to take this chalice away. His emotions were so intense that the scriptures tell us that big drops of blood dripped from His body like sweat...so intense were his feelings; Jesus, however, left that dark void and turned to His will. With utter surrender, he replied, "Yet, not as I will but as you will" (Matthew. 25:39).

This whole question of being peaceful involves a complete trust in God, a complete surrender to his plans. This is no small task; for many of us, letting go and letting God seems, at times, to be an impossible task. We want to be in control; we want to arrange everything our way. This Beatitude can help us to take little steps every day to become always more surrendered to all that the Father has planned for us. We can train ourselves in this by making little acts of surrender all through the day: we were hoping to have an outdoor picnic and the rain has started, we wanted to get home early from work to plan an evening with close friends and we are stuck in traffic. Each time we make a gentle surrender to these little annoyances, we strengthen our will and it becomes more and more capable of accepting a really difficult and challenging situation.

## Eighth Blessing

***Blessed are those who are persecuted for the sake of righteousness for theirs is the kingdom of heaven.**()*

Because in this book, we have equated righteousness with holiness, we will continue to do it for this blessing. Jesus is blessing those who are persecuted because of their living out of holiness. Francis does not have a good deal to say about being persecuted, but his experience of being persecuted was immense. I will share some of this persecution with you, drawing especially from *St. Francis de Sales and His Friends* by Henry-Coüannier.

*In 1594, Francis volunteered to go to the Chablais region to attempt to convert the Calvinists and restore the territory to the Catholic faith that once existed there. It was a difficult and dangerous assignment because*

*Catholics were hated and persecuted by the Calvinists. When Francis arrived to begin this new task, the country had already been under Calvinist domination for 60 years. Francis and his cousin, Louis, together made the long trek to the Chablais, all on foot; they were to be housed in the mountain fortress of Allinges, which the Calvinists had never managed to capture. It was the only structure in which they could say daily Mass. They would visit the towns during the day and then return to the fortress each evening for safety. Francis preached his first homily on the first Sunday after his arrival. There were only a handful of people present: a few nervous Catholics and a few curious Calvinists. A meeting of those few Calvinists resulted in a law being promulgated forbidding any Calvinists to attend his Mass or listen to his homilies. Following the enactment of this law, the people of Thonon hurled hundreds of insults at him, calling him idolator, false prophet and canting humbug. The threat of death hung over him. When his father heard about this, he sent a servant to bring Francis home immediately. Of course, Francis refused to leave. His cousin left with the servant to try to appease Monsieur de Boisy. This, of course, left Francis to carry out the mission alone.*

*During that first winter an attack was made on Francis. On two or three occasions, a man lay in waiting for him at the roadside and would have killed him with one shot had his aim not missed. The fanatic was then convinced that this provost was protected by some mystic power and he never tried again.*

*On another occasion, Francis was alone in the woods at night and wolves began howling. He climbed a tree and attached himself with his cincture so that he would not fall asleep and fall out of the tree. In the morning, this motionless, half-frozen man was found by some passersby who felt sorry for him and carried him home to get him near a fire. In his very first year at the Chablais region, Francis managed to convert only one person.* (*St. Francis de Sales and His Friends*, excerpts Chapter 6, pp. 69-75).

Francis did indeed really experience terrible persecution. He also experienced hardship. *He would leave the fort very early each morning and stay out until midnight. When the snow was heavy, he would get chilblains and his swollen feet became chapped and split. His suffering doubled when evening came and he arrived back at the foot of Allinges after hours of walking. The stony, uneven path that climbs steeply for about three-quarters of a mile became practically impassible when it was frozen. Francis felt the blood soak little by little into his socks and sometimes the snow was tinted red with each step that he took. He would finish the last part on his hands and knees. The Baron who was in charge of the fort accused him of killing himself but Francis replied cheerfully that he would thus get more quickly into heaven.*

*With all his suffering and persecution and prayers, Francis, in the end had managed after four years to bring back many thousands of persons to the true Catholic faith and the whole Chablais region became famous for the fidelity of the people to their newly restored faith. (St. Francis de Sales and His Friends*, excerpts Chapter 6, pp. 72-75).

What can we learn from all this? We have someone who can assist us in standing firm when moments of persecution arrive. We may never actually experience persecution but we can keep ourselves spiritually prepared and ready to endure generously any form of persecution or hardship. If ever it does happen, remember to take hold of your heavenly Father's hand and re-read this Eighth Beatitude and you will find the strength you need.

And so, my dear friend, we have completed our study of the eight Beatitudes; we each possess a key to holiness now…the key is simply to live these Beatitudes in our everyday life: to be gentle of heart and a peace-maker, to walk through our mourning, to be pure of heart, to be poor in spirit, to walk through persecution and hardship, to be merciful and to hunger and thirst for holiness.

I am going to assume that some of you, perhaps each of you, who are reading this book have a deep yearning to lead a holy life, to be the saints we are called to be. Let's take some time to ponder this whole idea of holiness,

# What is holiness?

What does holiness look like? How does it play out in our everyday activities and encounters? What do we do differently when we are acting in holiness? Is there such a thing as false holiness?

Since this pursuit of holiness is so very important to what this book is about, I would like to introduce you to someone who can assist us in understanding Francis' thoughts on holiness. His name is Bernard Bangley, a renowned author and lecturer; he is a Protestant pastor who is deeply in love with the spirituality of St. Francis de Sales. Realizing that many people, especially young people, struggle with Francis' 17th century language, he has taken on the task of editing the writings of St. Francis de Sales, and putting them into a more readable style for us.

He assures us, and I have found it to be true, that his approach is to keep the content of the book entirely that of St. Francis de Sales. He introduces no ideas, no insights, or no metaphors of his own. He sees his work on the *Introduction to the Devout Life* to be an honest paraphrase. I have personally come to treasure his writings and find that when I have read them, I actually understand the original 17$^{th}$ century piece more accurately. You will now be reading the *Introduction to the Devout Life* as interpreted by Bernard Bangley. I think you will enjoy the experience.

St. Francis de Sales wrote a wonderful book on holiness, which you now recognize as the *Introduction to the Devout Life*. He starts his guidance into holiness with a beautiful preface; I have chosen the excerpts that I think will benefit you the most.

# Introduction to the Devout Life

Preface by the St. Francis de Sales

*With flowers from the same garden, a flower arranger can create many different designs. This book contains nothing that has not already been said by others. I have picked the same flowers; the difference is in the way I present them.*

*Most devotional guides are prepared for individuals who are living a sheltered life apart from the everyday world. I want to teach the practice of devotion to ordinary people who work in a secular environment and live in town with their families.*

*Some may think that this is not possible. It is certainly not easy, but it can be done. This book is presented as a guide to anyone, in any situation, who wants to live a life of devotion to God.*

*As I wrote, I did not think of myself as addressing a large crowd but as talking quietly with one person. Because I know this will reach many souls, I invented a nickname representing an individual who seeks to love God through a life of devotion: Philothea means a lover of God.*

*I admit I am teaching before I am fully competent. It is my hope that the devotion I wish to instill in others may also grow in me.*

Annecy, St. Magdalene's Day, 1608

*(Introduction to the Devout Life, as interpreted by Bernard Bangley*, excerpts from the Preface.)

And now, we begin the journey into holiness as envisioned by St. Francis de Sales. Read his words prayerfully, and imagine them as being directed entirely to you. Let Francis touch your very heart. Remember that each time Francis uses the word *devout* he is referring to holiness.

It is my hope that the Beatitudes showed us how holiness is lived out; what I want to do now is to have St. Francis teach us what is not real holiness, so that we can begin the journey with a good understanding of authentic holiness and avoid any of the pitfalls of deception and misunderstanding.

The Pharisees in the time of Jesus, for example, considered themselves holy and upright leaders. The beautiful parable of the Pharisee and the Tax Collector praying in the temple is a lesson for all of us. The Pharisee prayed, and fasted, and tithed, all very holy actions. The pitfall was in the fact that he proclaimed his holiness to God; he was almost bragging in his prayer. The Tax Collector did not even dare to lift his head; he just prayed: "O God, be merciful to me; I am a sinner" (Luke 18:14). Jesus makes it clear which one went home justified. Let us listen attentively as St. Francis describes counterfeit holiness. Here is what he has to say:

*True devotion must be sought among many counterfeits. People naturally think their way is best. The person who fasts thinks this makes him very devout, even though he may harbor hatred in his heart. Another is a total abstainer from drink who tricks and cheats his neighbor, drinking, as it were, his neighbor's blood. Another is sure he is devout because he says many prayers and yet his language is arrogant and abrasive at home and at work. Another forgives his enemies but doesn't pay his bills. All these could be thought of as devout, but they are not. They only hint at devotion.*

*A person who is recovering from sickness walks only as much as is necessary. The pace is slow and hesitant. Anyone freshly starting on the path of devotion will also be limping. Eventually, like someone who is in good health, you will be walking, running, leaping toward God. "I run in the path of your commands, for you have set my heart free" (Psalm 119:32).*

*Aristotle noticed that a bee can extract honey from a flower without harming the flower. It leaves them as fresh as it found them. Authentic devotion does even better. Not only does it not interfere with earning a living, it also makes your work more effective. The same way a stone's particular color and pattern shines when moistened with honey, your occupation will be beautified and enhanced by your devotional life. Love at home will deepen. Being a parent will become more manageable. Any service you render will be more honest and faithful. Every job you do will be more enjoyable.*

*If you are very serious about this, it is important for you to find a good spiritual director, a faithful friend who can guide you along the proper path. "Faithful friends are beyond price; no amount can balance their worth. Faithful friends are life-saving medicine; and those who fear the Lord will find them"* (Sirach 6:14-16). *(Introduction to the Devout Life, as interpreted by Bernard Bangley*, excerpts from: Chapter 1, Instructions for Beginning to Fully Living the Devout Life).

My dear friend, I hope you have learned much from these excerpts from the *Introduction to the Devout Life.* I hope that each of us now possesses a good understanding of authentic holiness. Authentic holiness can be narrowed down to a deep and loving relationship with God and a generous and loving service to each neighbor. If those two things are in place, we are on the right path.

For myself, I get very uncomfortable when the habit I wear, for too many people, is supposedly a proof of my holiness. It is simply not true. The habit is a wonderful witness to my vocation, but I am just as capable of sinning as any other person. I am fully aware of my weaknesses, which is why I want to take this walk with you. I want to hold those keys to holiness with reverence and walk steadily each day on the journey to holiness.

We do have one small item to attend to: we listened to St. Francis on what holiness is *not*. I think it would be good if we close with an understanding of what authentic holiness really means.

First, if you are attempting to live out the beatitudes, my friend, then that is holiness; the pure of heart, the merciful, the poor in spirit, etc. are all indicators of holiness. However, the real test of holiness - authentic, contagious, joyful holiness, is this: holiness is pure and simple, doing the will of the Father. Francis states it very clearly:

*We must look to what God wills, and discerning His will we must attempt to fulfill it cheerfully, or at least courageously. Not only that, but we must love this Will of God and the obligation which results from it, even were we to herd swine all our lives and to do the most abject things in the world. Whatever service God asks of us, ought to be all one to us. Here is the very bull's eye of perfection, at which we all ought to aim, and whoever approaches it the nearest is the winner of the prize. (Golden Counsels, p. 20)*

Now the work begins, if your desire for holiness is still strong and vibrant. I strongly suggest that you use the *Golden Counsels* as a daily reference on this journey; the beauty of the *Counsels* is that they contain little pieces of advice and encouragement, little nuggets of wisdom on every imaginable Salesian topic. I think you will find them to be of great help in your journey. They can be found on several Salesian websites and are very inexpensive. Also, keep *Salesian Pearls of Wisdom* and *Living the Beatitudes* at hand. Open them to a section you are seeking or simply let the Holy Spirit direct you as you randomly open a page and choose a paragraph to read. The Holy Spirit will often communicate to us when we open a book to an unplanned page.

It gives him a marvelous opportunity to play an active part in our journey toward holiness.

I will be carrying you daily in prayer and I ask the same! May God's blessings be showered on our path to holiness!

I am as near as SrJohnMarie@mountaviat.org

I would be delighted to hear from you.

*We are companions on the journey!*

## Cited Works

De Sales, St. Francis. *Introduction to the Devout Life.* New York: Vintage, 2002.

DeSales, Francis, *Introduction to the Devout Life, as interpreted by Bernard Bangley.* Shaw Books, 1st edition, Colorado, 2002.

Golden Counsels of Saint Francis de Sales. Trans. Peronne Marie Thiert. Eds. Mary Paula McCarthy and Mary Grace McCormick. [St. Louis: Monastery of the Visitation], 1992.

Henry-Coüannier, Maurice. *St. Francis de Sales and His Friends.* Trans. Veronica Morrow. 2nd edition, Alba House, NY, 1973.

*New American Bible*, 4th Edition. St. Benedict Press. North Carolina, 2008.

Ratzinger, Joseph. *Jesus of Nazareth: from the Baptism in the Jordan to the Transfiguration.* Kindle ed. New York: random House, 2007.